JEANETTE WINTER

BIBLIOBURRO

a true story from colombia

BEACH LANE BOOKS • New York London Toronto Sydney

BEACH LANE BOOKS

An imprint of Simon & Schuster Children's Publishing Division

1230 Avenue of the Americas, New York, New York 10020

Copyright © 2010 by Jeanette Winter

Beach Lane Books is a trademark of Simon & Schuster, Inc.

For information about special discounts for bulk purchases,
please contact Simon & Schuster Special Sales at 1-866-506-1949
or business@simonandschuster.com.

The Simon & Schuster Speakers Bureau can bring authors
to your live event. For more information or to book an event,
contact the Simon & Schuster Speakers Bureau at 1-866-248-3049
or visit our website at www.simonspeakers.com.

Book design by Lauren Rille

The text for this book is set in MVB Grenadine.

The illustrations for this book are rendered in acrylic paint with pen and ink.

Manufactured in China

0316 SCP

10

Library of Congress Cataloging-in-Publication Data

Winter, Jeanette.

Biblioburro : a true story from Colombia / Jeanette Winter.—1st ed.

p. cm.

ISBN 978-1-4169-9778-8

1. Soriano, Luis—Juvenile literature. 2. Librarians—Colombia—Biography—Juvenile
literature. 3. Teachers—Colombia—Biography—Juvenile literature. 4. Biblioburro—
Juvenile literature. 5. Traveling libraries—Colombia—Juvenile literature. 6. Books and
reading—Colombia—Juvenile literature. I. Title.

Z720.S67W56 2010

020'.92—dc22

[B]

2009023559

For Demitri and Campbell

Deep in the jungles of Colombia,
there lives a man who loves books.

His name is Luis.

As soon as he reads one book, he brings home another. Soon the house is filled with books.

His wife, Diana, grumbles.

Luis thinks long and hard.

At last an idea pops into his head.

"I can bring my books into the faraway hills
to share with those who have none.

One burro could carry books,
and another burro could carry me—and more books!"

Luis buys two sturdy little burros.

He names them Alfa and Beto.

He builds crates to hang on their backs, and paints signs: BIBLIOBURRO— "The Burro Library."

Then Diana fills the crates with books.

Every week, Luis and Alfa and Beto set off across the countryside to faraway villages in the lonely hills.

This week they travel to El Tormento.

When the sun burns high in the sky,
Luis and the burros stop at a stream
to drink the cool water.
After they have their fill,
Beto balks.

Luis pulls and pulls on Beto's reins, but Beto won't budge.

The children are waiting for us!

At last the burro gives in and steps across the stream.

Deep in the hills, the path is lonelier than ever.
Bird songs are the only sounds they hear.
Then, from deep in the shadows,
a bandit leaps out!

"Please let us pass," Luis says.
"The children are waiting."
The bandit scowls at the books.
But he takes one and growls,
"Next time I want silver!"

The Biblioburro continues on its way
over the hills, until at last,
Luis sees houses below.
The children of El Tormento run to meet him.

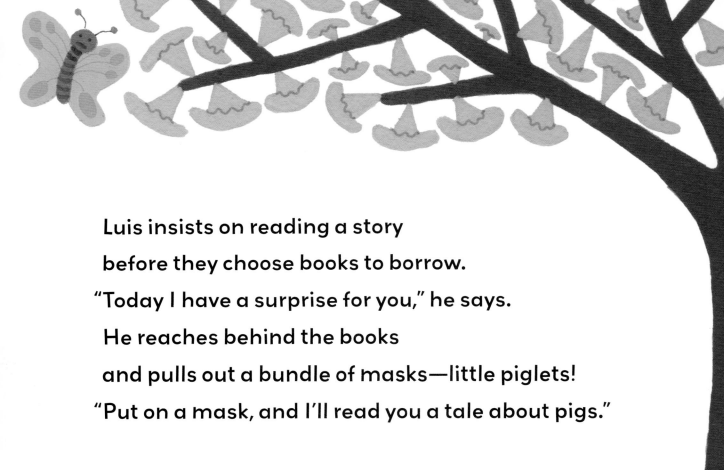

Luis insists on reading a story
before they choose books to borrow.
"Today I have a surprise for you," he says.
He reaches behind the books
and pulls out a bundle of masks—little piglets!
"Put on a mask, and I'll read you a tale about pigs."

When the story ends,
it's time for everyone
to choose a book.

The children hold their books close
as they say good-bye and walk home.

Luis and Alfa and Beto head back, over and around the hills, across the grasslands and streams, and into the sunset.

At home, Luis feeds his hungry burros.

And Diana feeds her hungry husband.

But then, instead of sleeping,

Luis picks up *his* book,

and reads deep into the night.

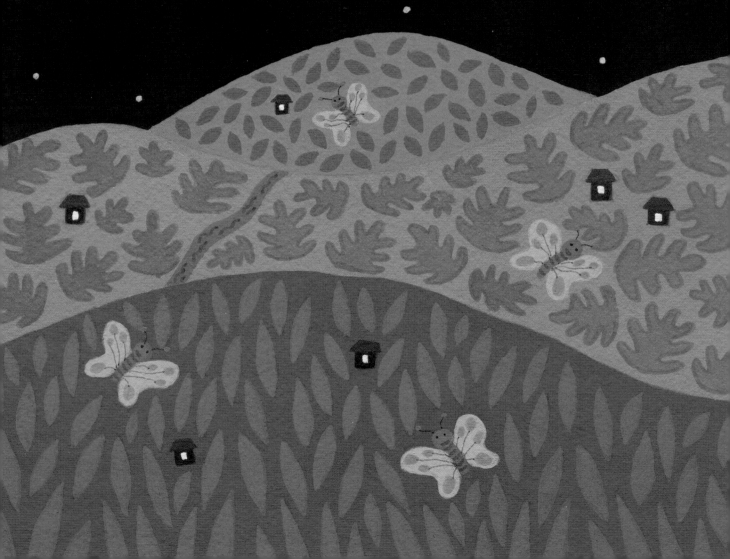

And far away in the hills, candles and lanterns burn

as the children read borrowed books deep into their night, too.

"People around here love stories. I'm trying to keep that spirit alive in my own way."—Luis Soriano

Biblioburro is based on the true story of Luis Soriano, who lives in La Gloria, a remote town in northern Colombia. An avid reader, Luis understood the transformative power of reading because of his experiences as a schoolteacher. He wanted to share his collection of books with the children and adults in the isolated villages in the distant hills, where books were scarce. Most houses had none.

Luis and his two burros began bringing books to the villages in 2000. He started with a collection of 70 books that has grown to over 4,800, mostly from donations. Now the Biblioburro travels to the hills every weekend. Three hundred people, more or less, look forward to borrowing the books Luis brings.

A small corner of the world is enriched.

—J. W.